FINISHING LINE PRESS

www.finishinglinepress.com

10048

poems by

Edward A. Dougherty

Finishing Line Press
Georgetown, Kentucky

10048

ACKNOWLEDGMENTS

Thank you to the editors of the following journals for choosing to publish
these poems:

Between the Lines—"Displacement"
Brain of Forgetting (Ireland)—first section of "Blowback" as "Going Back,
        Going Under"
The Whirlwind Review—"Project Safe Flight"
Mud Season Review—"Preserving the Fabric"
2 Bridges Review—"Gravity"
Up the River—"Dizzying Work"

Publisher: Leah Maines
Editor: Christen Kincaid
Cover Art: "Manhattan, View from Brooklyn, spring 2001."
        A daguerreotype. © 2015 Jerry Spagnoli
Author Photo: John Van Otterloo
Cover Design: Leah Huete

Printed in the USA on acid-free paper.
Order online: www.finishinglinepress.com
        also available on amazon.com

Author inquiries and mail orders:
Finishing Line Press
P. O. Box 1626
Georgetown, Kentucky 40324
U. S. A.

Table of Contents

❧

This collection benefitted from the encouragement of the Big Horn Writers Group (especially Margaret and Mary who read and commented on every page) and my brother, Chris. I also am grateful to George Guida, Martha Collins, John Bradley, Mike Aquilina, Gary Jansen, and Alan Catlin. Some of you believed in this book more fully than I dared to.

❧

For Beth.

"FROM the beginning
the collapse of the World Trade Center
has been a tale told in numbers as well as words…
One number gets little attention,
but it should not be ignored
in contemplating Lower Manhattan's future.
It is 10048.
That was the trade center's ZIP code."

—Clyde Haberman,
New York Times, November 14, 2003

"The skyscraper as symbol refuses to die."

—Ada Louise Huxtable
Wall Street Journal, September 17, 2001

Blowback

this goes into the bedrock of an island
and before the blueskies morning of September

an office building nine ten eleven stories high
could fit into the foundation hole the Ground Zero
        hole
the where-is-daddy hole the War on Terror hole

a hundred and forty six buildings
condemned and demolished to make room
what once stood is now gone for good
streets in lower Manhattan were blocked off
dug out and removed dump truck by dump
        truck
making real estate where once was only river

this goes way back and deep into the bedrock of a
        nation

        I I

"A group of mujahedeen
        who only a few years earlier
the US had armed

        with ground-to-air Stinger missiles,
grew bitter
        over American acts and policies

in the Gulf War....In 1993
        they bombed the World Trade center
and assassinated

several CIA employees
        as they waited at a traffic light
in Langley, Virginia...."

11

It was metal, the mountain.
So much concrete
vaporized, crushed to particles.

As I ran north, I tasted
the World Trade Center on my lips.

Gambits

in the time it takes to dial 911 on a cellphone,
to order a cup of french roast, two sugars, extra cream,
to decide on the green or blue blouse,
to log on and check the pileup of email,
in the amount of time it takes to breathe an Our
        Father,
to hail a cab and wait for it to pull up—
               Our building swayed a long way
               toward the Hudson River
               to the west   And then it stopped
               And then it came back to vertical
               And then there was no back and forth
               It didn't vibrate   It didn't oscillate
—you can see it frame-by-frame, watch it
        happening,
the ascending to vanishing, the blue, blue, the
        blue sky
and the tailfin all that's visible from the yet-
        smooth South Tower

             I I

As his driver plunged down Lexington,
a man can talk real estate
over bites of bagel

but still America means
one man, one vote,
which means equality

is borne on being born in these
United States: *so all you have to do,*
David, is buy the building yourself

then get Cedar Street
closed off
so you can build on both blocks.

William Zeckendorf made "grapefruit
from lemonade" from the optimism
of enterprise, juggling

thirty-five phone calls an hour
even in his Cadillac limo (this in 1955,
well before Bluetooth

but not long before bankruptcy
and anonymity capped off his riches-
to-rags story).

But roads require blacktop,
phone cables need steady
electrical pulses, and every tool

invents its inventor—
America created
Elisha Graves Otis:

the full-bearded showman
created the end of freefall
by inventing elevation, so confident, in fact,

that as he stood his uplifted ground,
he ordered an axman to cut the rope.
The car dropped

only inches, a distance you can bank on,
a distance that enabled
the scraping of the sky

so that Candice Tevere could step inside
an elevator the size of a living room
packed with fifty strangers

and zoom up to her 78th floor interview.
Upon arrival, doors zipping open,
phones ringing, she turned heel

and left, unwilling to work
in such an absurd place as the sky
over Lower Manhattan's checkerboard.

But this is chess
which means pawns
that need to be brokered

and resources rooked,
so Zeckendorf's plan
for a 'new corporate showplace'

needed relocating companies
to free up square after square
of square footage

in a complicated gambit he called
the Wall Street Maneuver
which positioned David Rockefeller

as a real player, his Chase Bank building
just the first foray
into these knight's errands.

I I

Fake ID fit him
                    as a fake contractor
and got him to the roof

but months of diagrams
                        got the crossbow
fit for the flight. In Richard Nixon's

August of Shame,
               Phillipe Petit, in a hard hat,
hauled all his gear

1000 feet up into the air,
                    his walking cable
assumed to be antenna equipment.

It took all night
                    to successfully arch the rope, pull
the cable, and ratchet it taut

so that at 7 am
                    as the first workers
were reaching the unfinished roof

he stepped into wind
                    to kneel midway,
then, improbably,

lay down, spine
                    to wire, face to sky,
and crowds to frenzy far below.

Seven crossings
                    he walked (45 minutes)
to help "frame them in glory"

glory
       in what lies between,
in all that is absent.

The Tallest Building in the World

In America, ambition fueled
moon-flight. What is it

about breaking the four minute mile
or scoring a 100 points in a game?

In the flea circus, the matchbook
is the tallest building in the world.

In the land of plenty, the home
of winning-isn't-a-sometime-thing,

a cut-throat culture stretches from Green Bay
to Pelican Bay, from Annapolis to Guantanamo,

from sea to purple mountain majesty.
So you'd think that when Minoru Yamasaki

agreed to design the World Trade Center,
everyone set out for the highest building ever.

But that came later. First, he strove
to 'scale it to the human being

so it will be inviting, friendly
and humane.'

'Warmth and human scale.'
Standards of the spirit.

What measures transcendence,
the depth of wisdom, or love's

tensile strength? These are never listed
in the *Guinness Book of World Records.*

This land and its people abide
and embody—*Do I contradict myself?*

Very well then.— these paradoxes,
their material and intangibility,

in our grief for towers now gone
and in wars that grind on.

| |

"the chain of events from the US
            arming and training of Afghan
and Al Qaeda mujahedeen

            to fight the Soviets in Afghanistan
to the Taliban and Al Qaeda
            and its international network

including fighters sent to
            Bosnia-Herzegovina
            Somalia
            Chechnya
            Central Asia
is direct."

| |

There were 40,000 doors
in the World Trade Center buildings

            Each door is a frame
                        each frame a cut

                        each cut a hand
            each hand a story

And like molten steel or liquid glass
into that hole America poured story after story

Magnetism

McKinsey & Co., consultants, in 1959
determined

there was no sense
in constructing a World Trade Center

> (1939: 'world peace through trade')

and certainly not in lower Manhattan

> *("why would anyone suffer*
> *the 'personal inconvenience'*
> *of moving downtown?")*

unless

> (America—land of the sweet
> unless, the deal-breaker's
> breakthrough)

unless it was 'unusual in nature'
'spectacular in proportion'
'an irresistible magnet'

| |

When the gym doors
                    burst open like milkweed
the cheerleaders kept on pom-pomming

but a ripple of bated breath
                    then murmuring
moved through the crowd. Five men

flapped
        as they streaked in a lazy
naked arc, bare feet slapping hardwood,

through center court,
                        the top of the key,
down the lane, and out the far doors

to fall in a jumble
                    in a waiting car. That fleshpile
in the backseat

and in the gymnasium
                        that hesitated hush, that gaping,
are images that endure.

Another kind of adventurism
                              marked that era.
Cartoonish in scale, George Willig

took a personal day from work,
                                George Willig
'a toymaker from Brooklyn'

equipped with foot grips
                          of his own fashioning
scaled the face of the South Tower.

Officers met him at the top,
                              congratulated him,
asked for an autograph,

then arrested him.
                    Willig's fine for trespassing
was reduced to a dollar and ten cents,

a penny a floor. Thanks
                        to Willig and Pettit,
an urban sport was born—

it pitted man
              against man-made structures.
Called *buildering,*

it enticed city rock climbers,
                       high-wire
aerialists, wall walkers all to summit

clock towers and offices,
                   anything ascending sky.
Officials at the WTC were not "overly joyful"

over this
        this "faddism"—they tightened up
security against 'threats to safety.'

        II

In February, 2002, five months after,
ruins smoldering,
a hundred feet down, bedrock was again struck,
finding what the city, what the island rests upon.

A physician in the World Trade neighborhood
that Tuesday never returned. Struck by debris?
drawn in to rescue? or did he take the chaos
as opportunity to step off the wire

and walk into another life, another identity?
At FreshKills, a gashed-open globe
contains a desk, there's a phone ringing
but no voice when answered,

there's a girder gone molten—*how hot's*
that got to get?—and now solid again
though twisted, of course. People say it's like
Hiroshima, only smaller, and now

over, but we still called 16 acres of urban wreckage
Ground Zero. Like filings, all of New York
and the rest of the world
we are drawn now

to where we all are resident
and there become witness and historian,
and there gather to take the vow:
                        'we will not repeat the evil'

Foursquare

It is my duty to God
shed his grace on
my responsibility to examine America
the Beautiful from inside
its trusses and knuckles, its glass,
its steel—

       American Steel, Gainsville, VA
       where Atlas Machine & Iron Works spun metal
       into base columns

              40 feet long, some 4 feet thick
              each 60 tons

       Dreier Steel on Long Island
       manufactured grilling, great metal feet
       for the whole structure to stand on

       Seattle, WA: Pacific Car and Foundry
       St. Louis: Laclade Steel (32,000 trusses)
       LA: Stanray Pacific

—my obligation to reassemble the materials, trace
the elements, to ride the elevators down,
to stomp schist,
and feel the earth below.

              I I

David Rockefeller's chief aides
headed off McKinsey & Co's 1959 report.
McKinsey was told

       You better stand there and say
       foursquare, we are for this,
       we think this is a good idea…
       There is going to be no concern.
       That is what you are going to say.

So the press conference in January 1960
was lovely New York theater:

in a jet age that shrinks the globe

the exchange of goods

the standard of living

the poor of many nations

Not all suspended disbelief, though.
Wrangling, in public and in boardrooms,
in courts and from podiums, went on
throughout the decade, even as the advisers in
        Vietnam
became soldiers and the casualties became
        unbearable...

1966—"Who's afraid of the big, bad buildings?"
asked Ada Louise Huxtable in the *New York Times:*
        "The trade center towers could be
        the start of a new skyscraper age
        or the biggest tombstone in the world."

1968—Lawrence Wien and his Committee
for a Reasonable World Trade Center
bought newspaper space to warn
that the "potential hazard
is staggering. Unfortunately we rarely recognize
how serious these problems are until
it's too late to do anything."
                In their ad,
a hand-drawn commercial airliner
cruises due south over Manhattan
about to slam the North Tower.

11

The shop owners of Radio Row
buried Mr. Small Businessman.
The power of eminent domain
was used to close and move them,
to shuffle them off to wherever.

They hoisted a flimsy, symbolic coffin
on their individual, human shoulders
to parade down street after street.
In the legers of the real,
how do we account for symbols,

for the single door with a single name
etched into its tiny, functional plate,
for the single shop, closed to clear land
in favor of prosperity (not theirs, of course)
and the idea of peace through commerce?

Displacement

'The lines between *military & civilian*
       targets, between military & civilian
populations had been erased

during the aerial bombings of WWII.
       This is not what is new
since September 11.

The bombings of London by the Nazis
       & of Dresden,
Hiroshima, and Nagasaki by the Allies

dramatically crossed the line
       between military & civilian targets
in modern war.

[This is not what is new since September 11.]

The Algerian Resistance against the French
       aimed at destroying
the *normalcy of everyday life*

by blowing up French residents of Algiers
       in cafés, markets, & train stations,
reminding them not only

they were the enemy
       but there could be no "normal life"
[What is new since September 11?]

              I I

Taped to mailboxes, curved around lamp posts,
slapped up on any flat wall or window,
even on cars parked long enough,

the faces, the lost faces, disappeared
and longed for, the faces stared out at the as-yet-
still-live ones who passed the passing.

Remember how candles pooled and flickered
under flowers that laced chain link
and how on the fence was a photo:

a white-veiled woman enwrapped
by her tuxedoed groom, and you couldn't
you couldn't tell who was missing and who

who was yearning, so you'd read the name
and learn she worked for Cantnor
up on the 90-something floor. Maybe the husband

and their two little girls photocopied
these sheets and, stapler and tape in hand,
walked street after street, glad

at least to be active in that awful waiting,
knowing and not wanting to know.
This was in the days we lined up for hours

to donate blood, remember? Blood
that was never needed. Of course
you don't. —We're ghosts talking to ghosts.

Before they footnote it, Cantor Fitzgerald,
a bond-trading firm, lost 700 out of 1000 employees.
Its offices occupied floors 101

through 105 of the North Tower,
the one struck first by American
Flight 11 at 8:46 am.

Poetry pours out through the net
of explanation. Have you seen
Amy O'Doherty? Adriane Scibotta?

Chris Kirby, 152lbs, blue eyes, a carpenter…
Tonyell McDay, ruby ring on left pinky finger…
Colleen Supinski, large blue eyes…

Francis (goes by Frank or Fran)—
two tattoos: one a Shamrock
in Irish flag colors over "Mom"

in the middle of his left arm,
and on his right
the kanji for "Mother."

                    | |

That region of lower Manhattan
had some things going on, remember,
so this was no simple move-along order,
night-sticking a sleeping vagabond's
bare and gnarled feet. We're talking
more than 100 residents, and employees
—thousands and thousands worked
in luncheonettes and haberdasheries,
flower shops, clothing stores, and grocers
            Cantor the Cabinet King
            Courtesy Sandwich Shop
            Oscar Nadel of Oscar's
                        Radio Shop and
                        Oscar's Radio & TV:
                                This is not some foreign country
                                where the government
                                can come in and just take
                                a man's business.
Businessmen were offered a flat rate
—mortgaged to the limit? booming income?

got the business forty-some years ago
from your pop?— $3000 bucks,
no more, no less. Take it or take it.

The 1916 zoning laws were revised
in 1961, an elegant Möbius strip of numerology
that allowed for an unprecedented tower-
in-a-plaza design based, of course, on precedent:
David Rockefeller's Chase Manhattan Bank gambit.

Still, in America, one man gets
one voice which he can shout into a bullhorn
because he's got rights. Unless,
unless, he runs into eminent domain:

> 'the public
> importance of
> piers
> markets
> slum clearance
> even   aesthetic
>   improvements'

> NY Court of Appeals Judge
> Adrian Burke sets us straight:

> 'public purpose
> justifies
> condemnation'

And in a jet age
a port needs no water
to create displacement

Descent

I was standing in front of the hotel. I'm a doorman
        I was in line at Starbucks
        I was in Ms. McKenna's third grade class
        I was at Mass
        I was sleeping when the phone rang

Is the point that tips forward
into a new era where we stood so that

          time
          becomes

location, a footprint on earth,
a place once functional, once measurable
square footage tallied as real estate as

          intersection
          becomes

symbol

          8:46 → 10:29
          9:03 →   9:50
             10 : 03

        I was waiting a table
        at a restaurant in Soho
        and I literally saw a
        it seemed to be a
        small plane it looked like it
        bounced off the building
        and then
        I just saw a huge ball of fire on top of the building…

When did you realize it was deliberate?

How many hours of TV did you watch?

Who did you know and why were they there?

For how many days did you sleepwalk?

Who saved your life, who pressed your body
to theirs, who held you in balance?

| |

in the stairwell from the 70th floor

"The building, this enormous
skyscraper, this national monument
swayed back and forth

This is it I thought *Get ready
to go down with the ship.*
My body and mind went numb

I didn't start praying
I didn't have visions of childhood
I didn't see my life flash before my eyes

I went into this white
arctic zone   I don't know what it was
I was blank   I was blank   I was nothing

Time had vanished
There was no time
There was only descent

There was only counting
and waiting and counting,
circling around again and again..."

| |

> *"Maybe the walls of Jericho fell down*
> *because they weren't built on good foundations."*
> —John Kyle, Chief Engineer at the Port Authority

The shelf runs south, and as it runs
it sinks farther and farther under Lower Manhattan,
and the bedrock stretches under Staten Island
and through New Jersey. This is the foundation
of the foundation, like liberty under laws.

For the World Trade Center, they had to dig out
all the layers of accumulated landfill—
old bricks and rubble, hand-forged nails,
a century-old slipper, cannonballs
and a cannon muzzle, several clay pipes,
ancient anchors, including a 1000-pound hulk
it took nineteen men to haul out—
the leavings of Colonial, Federal, and all our other
previous versions, our neighbors in time,

then they dug out the oozy black mud,
river silt, Hudson River silt, sediment
once suspended in currents and tides
that settled out and layered down
to coat docks and whole sunken ships,

then came bull's liver, yards and yards
of the stuff—maybe another story's worth—
red sand that fills in as you dig it out,
like a beach hole that gets wider
but only slowly goes deeper,

next comes clay, hardpan
packed by glaciers and their boulders,
now we're time traveling, 10,000 years,

and finally,
below the hardpan and quicksand of bull's liver,
and under the oddments of garbage till,
finally, the backbone of the island:
where there is no under, no further back,
where the country is no more,
where we are still the land's
before the land is ours.

Imagination, And Its Limits

It's a system of words, the rule of law.
Once lawyers define 'public purpose'
and 'eminent domain,' they construct
their own towers, and other lawyers
contest that this or that enterprise
can be housed in its confines.
Politics is politics, the way
you can't fight City Hall, the Port Authority
and the NY Court of Appeals
but politics is road work, too.

Shopowners took to the streets,
as in 'street theatre', with bullhorns
and mock funerals, a show
not of force but conviction, a gesture
for sympathy. And sympathy scales
any enterprise to the human.

Since city government has jurisdiction
over the space between one curb and another,
that's power. You gotta figure
who decides what:
1966: new mayor, new gambit.

He works both words and roads.
Calls public meetings
on the trade center proposal
and takes a lighter to the permits
the Port Authority needs
to use, destroy, or build
a single roadway
in the great City of New York.

| |

It was heat, not impact.
Melting, not velocity.

Fuel, not airspeed.
Then mass rode gravity.

Engineers imagined airliners,
of course; the towers
were designed to absorb
and withstand concussions

but imagining couldn't account
for capacity, in passengers
and so in fuel, for the scale
of 21st century (barely)

aircraft. Imagination
begins somewhere; its limits
are hidden until, like glass,
they're breached.

From his office just streets away,
structural engineer, Les
Robertson witnessed
his creation's fate. *Yes*, he says,

*we watched it, and you could
reach out—*
his hand goes to the window
and the gap

in the skyline
*—and touch it.
But there was nothing
you could do.*

11

February 26, 1993.
Because we didn't notice,

didn't heed, didn't stop:
Six dead.

Rented vans. Urea Nitrate,
a source of fertilizer, to feed
crops. Or fuel poison.
The theory: one tower

tripped from underground
(bomb in the parking garage)
would topple the other.
But the van wasn't packed

to its one-ton capacity,
the fire consumed
the sodium cyanide.
My greatest regret,

said Ramzi Ahmed Yousef,
was not using
enough explosive.
Only six dead.

Sound Waves

Do you remember the stillness
          (despite the always-on
          I-can't-take-it-anymore
          buildings-coming-down news)
the empty skies—
four days
no flights.

Schools closed. Football games canceled.
Hollywood halted filming, the Emmy's postponed.
Internet sites crashed.

From a NYC police copter
one witness reported:
a vast cloud of smoke, dust
and debris engulfed
the financial district.

Buildings disappeared
          boats fled the scene.

There was silence.

In the helicopter
—the collapse, the cloud
made no sound,

and no one spoke.

| |

Harry Druding
raised the four foot rebar
—equipment shut off
so all could listen
to the stone's voice.

As much as sixty feet
below street level, workmen
stuck bedrock, then blasted
to reach steadier stuff.
When solid layers
revealed themselves,
they chiseled.

Now they were poised.
Waiting. Motionless.
Gaps and faults
would register
in muffing tones:

Druding swung
and the metal made
a sweet ping

on which all the concrete,
all the steel, aluminum,
and each of the 43,600 windows
would rest. Listen:

‖

Overhead, a roaring,
and it got closer and closer.

In the walls, in the skewed building—
a grinding, a squealing,
something I never heard
even in the worst storm.

When the tower righted itself
there was a bubble—no fire alarm,
no announcement on the intercom. Nothing.
Just that bubble of quiet.
Which was worse.

I heard one of the firefighters mumble,
"We've got jumpers."

Every half a minute, oh God,
the bodies never stopped.
Every thirty seconds
the horrible crushing sound
echoed through the lobby.

It was a freight train,
the sound twisting steel makes
straining to hold
against the stress within it.

The undercover cop was muttering,
"This thing could go, this thing
could go, this thing could go."

Sirens. Coming from everywhere.
Vanishing in the distance.

The sound of no dial tone.
Every pay phone I tried.

Hacking. Everyone coughing
through handkerchiefs and shirtsleeves,
coughing their lungs out.

"You believe this?
No way am I ready for this."
Then the sergeant shouted, "Go, go, go!"

The faraway sound, like someone
was trying to reach me,
but it was me, saying *I gotta
get out of here. I gotta find my wife.*

Weeks later, the CEO's voice over
the airline company's intercom
asking for a moment of silence.

Echoes

In the days after, not yet called post-anything,
days that were still just our lives, days

of slow walking
and sleep walking,

there was a crossing over—
we passed between the abstract

(danger of terrorism) into the actual,
but such lines were not so much crossed

as blurred or bent into unreal zones
where the actual never felt so disembodied—

days of slow-walking lines of uniforms,
a procession in silence, the stone

of their faces eroded, days haunted
by the wheeling blare of bagpipes

(a sound that for some still echo the sound
of those days). The sirens, too, were strange:

after John McLoughlin, Port Authority
police officer, was pulled alive

from the Pile a day later,
"ambulances rushed in

but did not rush out."
Funeral after funeral

followed those autumn days,
the line unending.

In actuality, it ended.

| |

Mornings, elevator doors split open
    Salaam Aleichem
    Peace be upon you
a construction worker might greet
an electrician, but the chorus back
    Aleichem salaam
came from the suits too.

      Financial execs, investment
          bankers, insurance brokers

            from Jakarta and Abu Dabbi,
            Dubai and Manchester,

        all in New York
    for the rituals of business

and all passed through those elevators
to join the enterprise
of shrinking the globe through trade.
And so achieve peace.

Many found their way to the Prayer Room
on the 17th floor of the South Tower,
a room set aside for a different ritual:

      first in a small washroom
          cleansing hands, face, and feet

          and then to face east
    and intone the *salat* prayer

| |

Some events contain
their own hollow   *Hello?*
      space to savor
      space to mourn

contain their own echo   *No,*
waves rolling back
to answer feeling
for feeling

How much is a life worth   *life's worse—*
when it's gone?

If you listen too hard
to money, it's whisper   *its*
can break stone.   *ache*

We say it's cold   *is old…*
we say it's hard
but money's as much
an idea as a koan

How much comfort   *Comfort?*
does 1000 dollars bring?

30 years old. Stockbroker.   *4.3*
Survived by a wife and two children.   *million?*

Janitor. 55.   *540*
Wife, and an ex, three children.   *thousand?*

Having an economic scale
says the electrician's father
is a disgrace.

This is awful
the lawyer declaims *forcing*   Lame
a change in lifestyle
which the law   law.
is supposed to prevent.

Drill down through any life's   I
detritus, hope to hit
bedrock   *rock*
but instead we find   *in*
there are empty spaces,   *empty*
the earth's
open arms.   *arms.*

All are equal before
the still-smooth bedding,
the empty seat at the table.

The Special master of the Victims'
Compensation Fund knows   *No*
all men   *one.*
are created equal

but also knows   *No*
under New York law   *wonder*
the father of the deceased   *father*
is entitled   *is*
to zero damages   *—oh*
(unless dependent)

and he knows in court
plaintiffs   *his*
have to prove fault

and so uses another calculus: *loss*

insurance payouts are deducted,
claims capped,   *aims*

and all parties
agree—   *a reed*
keep this thing out of the courts.

It's still the wrong economy,   *(me)*
using the wrong table:

    under our feet   *under*
    water seeks the lowest point   *water.*
    seeks to fill
    and filling

    overflows.

Negative Damping

The experiment was simple:
tunnel, model of New York
(to scale), and wind,
wind made by a four-blade
WWII fighter plane propeller.

The balsa wood towers
(two feet, eight inches high)
were painted white, ghost blocks
of what did not yet exist
and does not again, except
in imagination. Turn
the towers any which way
and the result's the same:

bring on a good gale, a hurricane, say,
in off the Atlantic, raising chop
on the surface of the Hudson,
each wave making its own
turbulence, each Brooklyn building
and each Manhattan structure
creating its own drag,
but the balsa,

the only material light enough,
flexible enough to mimic
the WTC designs at this scale,
the balsa wood towers
teetered and cycled, wobbling
in synchronized
oscillations. First one, then the other,
then returning to a double sway.

500 : 1   means
the tips of the buildings
would swing in the real world
twenty

to forty feet.
Where your office is,
it would not be.

‖

a single 70-story tower
on a 3-story 'platform'
$250 million
13.5 acres
all along the docks of the East River

'a port without water"
a port that needed authority
to raze that kind of space in Manhattan

The Port Authority of New York
(and New Jersey) had to sell
two state legislatures as well as city officials
on the scheme and still avoid
the mass transit business.
It helped that Nelson Rockefeller was governor.

Jersey nodded finally when the deal
included the Hudson *&* Manhattan
Railroad terminal—
twenty-two story twins
whose ship had sailed into a future
without dray horses, though commuters
still need passage into the city,
so the whole trade complex
had to march west on Fulton Street,
the footprint stomping the road itself out
along with 3 blocks of Dey, Cortlandt,
Washington, and Greenwich

Now near the Hudson
we're looking at 13 blocks
covering 16 acres
at a proposed cost of $470 million

| |

Air strike and drone attack,
missiles zero in on the convoy
crossing the only road in the high desert
          calibrate
               distance, project
                     the progress the vehicle
            will make
        in elapsed time

acting on intelligence
acting on intelligence

Negative damping, engineers call it when wind force,
diverted by a solid face, breaks off the surface
and spins away, curling, twisting into a vortex,
a small tornado pulling the form that parted it,
drawing the bridge span, drawing the skyscraper,
and getting it to sway, to oscillate.

Negative damping, they call it, where *damp*
means to pat down
and so diminish
some action, *settle down, there,*
easy—hands up, voice calm—*easy,*
intentions clean and simple, every
                 movement
                 deliberate
but this damping is *negative*, a twist
of language where diminishment
is opposed so motion increases
or resentment grows

when the missile blackens the roadway
with blood-burned scrap metal, the bodies
of villagers, say, traveling to a funeral
or a relative's birthday
                          collateral damage
they call it, apologizing, *we acted*
on intelligence, intelligence
wrong not the act, as wind
picks up dust and swirls it,
a circling motion for the story
to pass now lip to ear, lip to ear...

Corrugated

Dear friends, denied seats on the same flight,
said their goodbyes at Boston's airport, then
      boarded:

one on American, the other on United.
American, United. Untied later, Americans

taped flags to brick walls, attached them
to car windows, tied them to fences on
      overpasses.

Stars and Stripes forever. Notes posted
above flowers, photos, more Old Glories—
      Remember not

the horrors, one sign read, *only the heroism.*
These were prayers, physical psalms rising to heaven

out of dusty questions: Can we know humanity
without knowing grief? The word *al Qaeda*

means *the base* or *foundation,* but there's something
deeper down, isn't there? When does night end

and day begin? Their mantra was 'the necessary
permits the forbidden.' Our refrain was a slogan

I misremember as *These colors do not bleed,*
so the flag's red stands stark in my mind against sky
      blue.

The stars' bright blaze asks, Can we mourn
and seek revenge simultaneously?

We do it all the time. Those aren't the poles that
      oppose.
Grief fuels rage, the desire to destroy and make
      bleed.

Can we seek revenge and make justice? Morning
        was still dark
as passengers streamed toward Logan. Ruth
        Clifford McCort

and her daughter, Virginia, were headed to LA.
So was Ruth's best friend, Paige Mackel. Is our
        answer

our mourning? Something deeper, there must be
a foundation below the foundation, emptiness

folded within matter where all that's still possible
        moves,
where re-arrangements happen by happy
        chance,

where no future is fixed and no feeling final.
Ruth and her daughter boarded United Flight 175

which crashed into the South Tower. Ruth's
        brother,
Ronnie, dashed into the intersections that grid

Lower Manhattan, and phoned Ireland. Their
        brother there
worried about Ronnie's trip to New York,

neither of them aware of the fate of those above
        him.
Time corrugates to make space for unknowing,

for unlearning the obvious, like the
        difference
between friend and enemy, the living and the
        dead,

solid and fluid, past and passing.
Mohammed Atta's second piece of luggage from
        Portland

didn't make its connection, so officials found the
        handbook
which says, 'Angels are calling your name."

That bag circled the carousel for hours. And that's
        one ending
to the story. The other stays with the question

until the rabbi says night will not end
until our vision is keen enough

to look on the features of any man or any woman
and recognize a brother, a sister.

                    I I

"My initial reaction—
            this was not a war
but classic terrorist action

        unpredictable
only in choice of
        weapon
                    target
                        success
                            and impact

no enunciated political objective
no relationship between action and grievance
no distinction between military and civilian"

11

No photos, buddy, the officer commanded,
punching him in the shoulder,
This is a crime scene. Even so,
movie lights illuminated
the whole night:

amid the metal wreckage
of I-beams and twisted columns,
an odd collection of plastic cafeteria
and leather conference chairs,
there was an enormous book:

as many as ten stories of the building
were compressed into a foot-thick space.
Ignoring the cop's directive,
the photographer obeyed
the eternal command: *Take and read.*

He wandered all over the Pile
where the Bathtub's exposed wall
loomed again and the river
seeped through. Picture the fireman,
whose shift had ended but who couldn't leave:

"We're gardeners," he said still working his rake,
"in the gardens of the dead."

Gravity

1968. Year of the assassin.
Importing from Asia
body bags. One eye
trained on the ground,

the earth of which
we are made and
to which we return,
the other following

the train rail
down which dreams
and all that steel
chugged along.

Grillages were to be set
into trenches chiseled
three to four feet deep—
picture it:

men crawling over bedrock
too slick to stand,

picture it: an inspector slipped,
plunged into a pit,

leg and hip broken, imagine:
one man in that hole, one man hauled out

on a stretcher, one miniscule person,
one man in such vast emptiness.

II

It was Italians and Italian-speaking
Americans who engineered and drilled down through
fill, silt, and sand to slam into bedrock,
where they could find it.

After laboring 14-hour days, George Tamaro,
Jersey native, with a little one
on the way, routinely got roused
by phone calls. In his sleepless way,
he moved The Bathtub along.
Not a tub to soak in, this one
kept water out, sealing foundations
against the Hudson. A wall to encircle 11
of the westernmost acres.

Digging for a panel along Greenwich
(a part of which itself would float away,
sink in the river, and become
Battery Park City),
drilling didn't stop, all that air
where schist should be—

the underground cave
and neighboring hundred-foot valley
was hollowed by glacial streams
and the power of gravity—
though the watercourse
and ice sheets were gone.

We understand now what they couldn't then:
our dearest companion is the missing.

II

The falling man, the man on wire,
the vertical tension of the scale
and the physical tenderness
of the body, the individual life,

the individual man, falling
but in the photo hanging as if from a wire,
gravity's relentless, inevitable tension suspended;
the result: an odd tenderness

for the elegance of the image
and its gravity, as it hangs
in memory as if on a gallery wall,
the Tower's vertical body

framed in memory and in such artifacts,
their scale increasing as grave
as symbol, and yet there is more:
there is this individual feeling,

a feeling in the body, a tenderness
for another human being, a person—
and for a moment we remember
the elegant body of our kinship.

Domino Theory

'They came from the Kingdom
        that houses and protects
the holy places of Islam

        and it is at the same time
a filling station
        for the Western economy.

(source of one fifth of America's petroleum)

The goal was first
        clear Saudi Arabia
and its oil fields

        of American personnel
then, take over Pakistan
        and its atomic arsenal.

Acts of religious terror
        are not done for the sake
of farmers, workers,

        students
or oppressed
        and helpless people.

They are done
        in the name of God.
But God will not reply to them.'

II

As if from the white film
of atomized towers,
rescue cities sprouted up.

First, they were tarps,
stretched against rain; the exhausted
would sit a while, gasp oxygen

then head back in. We still expected,
still hoped. Tarps became tents,
then a wooden shack for firefighters,

some with windows. The most expansive
called the Taj Mahal
had showers, a dining room,

a place for massages.
But no one left the scene
without being hosed down.

An accidental beauty, moments
of random elegance: From the metal,
a flock of monarch butterflies rose.

Welders' blue *skoosh* of flame,
its hiss, the grind of cutters, the truck
and crane engines—the sounds

of deconstruction
were constant, unassembling
with precision, small explosions

whenever metal, removed,
made a pocket that got filled in
with oxygen. But then there were

puffs of silence: work stopped, workers
removed helmets, thus the living
honored the dead.

11

February 1993	World Trade Center, basement bomb so the towers would tip like dominos
(June 1993	Plan to explode and collapse two NYC traffic tunnels, the UN Building, and the NY offices of the FBI.)
(1994	Plot to hijack a dozen Manila Air jumbo jets, destroy them mid-flight)
1995	Attack on US troops in Riyadh, Saudi Arabia (35 dead)
1998	Simultaneous explosions at US embassies in Tanzania (10 dead) and Kenya (253 dead)
(New Year's Eve 1999	Attack planned on LA International Airport)
(January 2000	Plan to sink the USS *The Sullivans*, a US warship docked in Arden Harbor)
October 2000	USS Cole attacked, Arden Harbor (17 dead)
September 2001 ...	

Freefall

Down flight after flight,
she finally reached the lobby.
Sprinklers soaked her.
But then: behind
and beyond her:
a weird rumble:
nearly a third of a mile
of glass and metal:
the whole South Tower
coming down.
Second struck, first to fall.
So this is it, she thought,
this is the end. After walking
down all those stairs.
But then: a policeman
grabbed her, hauled her
downward again,
into the subway, the shuddering
crush all around now, down
as if into their own grave.

‖

I thought I was blind. The air blast
like a hurricane stormed through the concourse
and blew me to my knees, into water
and broken glass. When I opened my eyes:
I can't see anything anymore,
I heard my colleague call out.
Dust blackened the air.

‖

Cotton balls. It felt like
being stuffed with black cotton balls.

‖

Now that it wasn't a rescue mission,
all through the North Tower, the same command:
 "Get out! Get out!" Firefighters dropped gear,
reversed direction. Below the 96th floor
the building was evacuated.

"Clear out. Down now." Down,
winding around those same stairwells
they'd just mounted. At the 16th,
debris stopped them, wreckage
from the other building, "Stairwell B—let's move,
come on, let's move!"

At each level, open the door,
point bullhorn, shout, "Get out,"
The same ritual, into emptiness.
Until the 12th floor. There,
50 - 70 people sat in an office.
He couldn't believe his eyes.
What were they thinking?

Only then did he make out
the crutches and wheelchairs.

‖

The morning started out
hoping for the kind of day
you could repair lawnmowers
at the stationhouse.

‖

Tons, hundreds of tons reached
freefall speed, the velocity of a body,
tie pointing skyward
when the North Tower imploded.

And in the lobby, crushed girder
and twisted-but-intact beams
created a hollow, a cave
in the mountain of metal
where a handful of survivors
coughed, eyes stinging,
voices thinned by strain—
alive, they were alive
in a chamber made of chance.

The survivors found themselves
before anyone else found them
in a stairway jutting from rubble,
a capsule launched somehow
to the edge of ruins.
Everyone there was rescued.

11

The bodies on the ground
were not always motionless.

Diligence

To pilot a commercial airliner,
one needs to be part of a team
and work together well.

One must be dependable,
self-disciplined, a role model.
"Can the candidate take criticism?"

The owner of Florida
Flight Training called one terrorist
"the perfect candidate"—

helpful to others,
cheering up classmates
when they got down. They liked

having photos taken
with him. He was punctual,
always in a good mood.

‖

In small amounts, the money came in.
Into separate accounts
from separate points of origin.
No regular pattern. Perfect.

You can't get far down these streets
not-made-of-gold before *smack!*
running headlong and wallet-wise
into a bank. Go to Maine's
Acadia and listen
to the gravel crunch of Rockefeller's
carriage roads. Head to the Adirondacks
and walk through the Great Camps;
those rustic estates, which had electricity
before the surrounding towns,

were built for and staffed year-round
for the get-away of America's
captains of industry.

The money came in. Money
to rent an Altima
idling outside the Comfort Inn,
to pick up dinner at Pizza Hut,
to hold the apartment in San Diego
where the logistics team
slept on bare mattresses
and owned no other furniture,
through they carried briefcases
and took cell phone calls
as they ducked on occasion
into the limousine that came for them,
like bankers—strange, strange bankers.

And the money still came in. Money
to take a room at an EconoLodge
or disappear into well-off anonymity
behind the community's gated front,
to grab a copy of Microsoft's
Flight Simulator '98
or buy more Marlboro Lights for Atta
or purchase two first class
United tickets for $4,500
or tip the dancer
at the Olympia Garden Topless Club.

A young teller, counting wire transfers,
tallies them for account # 5730000 259 772,
a most unpoetic detail. The poetry
is in her diligence, the banality
of virtue.

11

Siad Jared learned to fly,
passed his pilot's test
without difficulty, but his other mission
for more than a year was to live
amid the enemy, cheerfully accept
instructions from him. He was to
get to know his enemy, party
with him, laugh with him
—and at the end
still be able to kill [him.]

Not the window washer
who'd left home in Jersey at 5am
to be at his glass on time;
not the Cantor secretary;
not Albero Dominquez, a passenger
from Sydney, Australia, father of four;

not any particular person, not the enemy
as an individual, only as narrative,
an abstraction
no number of dead
can make real.

Möbius Strip

Just before 10 am, the engine roar over Manhattan
was a terror in itself. It seemed trained on
the tallest building in the world, but watch time

as dates get muddled, more Möbius strip
than fluid progression. Time, the great snake,
bites its own tail so that July 28, 1945,

circles around to seem so like a September morning,
where one followed war, the other was prelude.
Just months before, the Navy man tipped back

the nurse in Times Square, that kiss so indelible,
so symbolic, so problematic, so American,
but come summer, twelve tons of B-25

collided with the Empire State Building, tearing a
                hole
20 by 18 feet through stone and steel.
Back then firefighters could ride elevators

to the 60th floor and extinguish the blaze in a half hour.
Nowadays, *You gotta be young in Manhattan,*
to fight fires, lugging a hundred pounds of gear

up into those flimsy glass towers, sometimes
all for a bag of burned popcorn, a wiring
                problem,
but once it was the real deal: a Boeing 767 weighs
                120 tons,

and carries 9000 gallons of, not gas, but jet fuel.

                ǁ

Up through the current
of office workers streaming down,

up the stairs, up and around
each flight, burdened
earthbound by oxygen tank,
coiled hose, bearing up, carrying
all that's needed, bearing it
upwards, so high
that if you stood forehead
to window glass
you'd gaze down at the blades
of a helicopter, that is, if you could
reach a window and if
there were a helicopter and if one
could swoop in onto the roof
and rescue those gathered,
but no way, not through
all that oily smoke roiling
up the building, a black
drape already unfurling
skywards, rolling over
and covering the roof
choking any who ascended,
waiting there as firefighters
climbed the stairs, the smoke-
choked columns within the core
of the tower, which smelled
like kerosene, but still
they kept climbing,
men in suits patting
him on the shoulder,
their hands red-raw,
all the while the burn
in his legs going numb
and the dry clamp
in his lungs squeezing
as he worked upward
but when he could,
he could look up, he'd watch

the soot-faced people, story
after story, pouring past,
each person, each
face, each person's face...

11

When they finally pried open
the elevator doors, they faced a wall.
There were no stops, no docks for this ferry
between the 44th and the 74th floors. In that vessel,

the acting director of the Port Authority
was stranded. He and five others faced the wall.
From their various stations, they had heard
the impact, felt the sway, and converged here,
hoping to head down and escape. But then
suspended in their flight
they had to tug the elevator doors open by hand.

The window washer had the tools of his trade,
so they scraped at sheetrock, jabbed
and gouged, knuckles bleeding, only to reveal
another layer. They kept at it. One, two,
three panels of sheetrock

before they could enlarge the tiny hole
made by the now-broken squeegee handle,
they kicked a passage
large enough for the smallest
to wriggle through. 2000 employees

of the Port Authority worked in the Towers,
a quarter of the whole company.
Not all had titles, carried briefcases,
held press conferences, but every person
has a history, and the ex-postal worker

had 61 years of it. On his way to work,
every morning, he'd stop at a foodtruck
to pick up breakfast
for himself and something
for a co-worker in a wheelchair.

Not only did he pass through that wall,
not only did he actually return—and with help—
not only were they delivered from their hold,
but this one, the smallest man,
birthed another version of himself,

one that lives on in the intricate anonymity
of any particular life.

The Afghan Trap

Take a small domed cage
suspended from a tiny pulley,
drop a silver ball down a long,
grooved slope, dinging a bell
along the way, and watch it
speed up for the jump,

so that for an instant, the metal sphere
doesn't touch any part
of the Goldberg contraption—will it sail
the gap? will it trip the lock
and drop the newfangled mousetrap?
will the unwitting prey wait that long?

These and other questions
hung in the calculating air, 1979,
as the Carter Administration constructed
The Afghan Trap, though we were after
far larger game than some pesky rodent:
we wanted to catch the lumbering bear

of the Soviet Union. No one wants
to poke directly at a baited bear,
so the Afghan Trap consisted of this:
gather and train Islamic fundamentalists
in Pakistan, then unleash them
on the communist puppet running Afghanistan

not to overthrow the government
(machinations now called
"regime change") but agitate and
destabilize, antagonize
just enough—that's the delicate part—
just enough to draw the Soviets

into their own debilitating Vietnam.
Like cartoon mice loosed in the circus

cause elephants to stand upright
on their yellow and blue risers, shrieking
and pulling up their costume skirts—
this was a gambit without regrets.

When questioned, in fact, in 1998,
former National Security Adviser
Zbigniew Brzesinski posed his own follow-up:
What is more important to the history
of the world? The Taliban
or the collapse of the Soviet Union?
Some stirred up Muslims or…

But why choose? A remarkable machine like this
could do both and still make it rain marshmallows.
Regret what? he asked. *Why all these questions.*
Lift the tiny cage and the crowd gasped
at the stone rubble of the Bamiyan Buddhas
and Fritz Koenig's gashed metal *Sphere.*

‖

"Anything can happen
        when human beings allow
ideology to trump

        their humanity, when they elevate
an idea
        above the lives of individuals.

Anything
        can happen, and too often
does."

‖

Did Mohammed Atta
smell of fruity Comfort Inn Botanical Shampoo
in the dark of morning
after showering in his non-smoking room
in Portland, Maine? We don't know.
But he was sure to follow the manual's instructions
to "not leave your house
unless you are washed and clean,
for the angels will forgive you
if you are clean." We do know
he left his house. That much, we know. That
and when they checked in,
they paid in full—$149.
They had an early flight,
so they'd be up and out.
Such strange courtesy.
What to do with such gestures?
How do we account for the fact
that one of the Strongmen,
whose task on the plane is clear
from his title, took in his hand
the motel keeper's hand,
thanked her, and said, "It was good
knowing you. You are a very good person."

Project Safe Flight

Before the site was a foundation hole
but after it was a construction site,
two residents did not wish to leave:

One gazed from his penthouse window
atop a five-story office building
at beloved river views.

The other, who had escaped
the about-to-be-demolished pet shop,
holed up in a beam-nest, raiding
area fruit stands to survive. The monkey
managed to elude workmen for months.

| |

"After September 12
           no one was found alive
and the dogs

           were distressed.
It became necessary
           to stage situations

where 'survivors'
           were found by the dogs
to keep up their morale."

| |

Following hour after exhausting hour,
they turned in flight, circling,
confused by lights not in the sky
but somehow in the sky nonetheless.
Drawn from millennial flyways, drawn
and disoriented, migrating birds
orbited two great hazards: light

and glass. Eventually,
some of these air travelers
descended into the city to land
and rest in trees and shrubs in planters.
Come dawn and the rising of the sun,
in the Trade Center's vast plaza,
they were trapped in a maze
of invisible walls and reflected shapes.
Birds battered the same windows.
At the base of the towers, volunteers
recovered hundreds of bodies.

The project, then, was simple: webcams
trained on the long vertical walls revealed
which floors remained illuminated (and so
attractive) and which windows
proved most dangerous. Tenants
were eager to help and the Port Authority
netted the insides of the glass.
In this way, the death toll was diminished.

Years later, after the towers were gone,
beams of light towered into the now-
disorienting space, and inside these bright shafts
white specks glittered. *It was hard,*
one witness said, *not to think of souls.*
In the dark of the moon, flocks
following the guidance of starlight
were bedazzled and caught up
in the brilliant memorial.

American Redstarts, Baltimore Orioles,
thrushes and warblers were released,
freed from their circling flight
when the lights were shut off.
Just twenty minutes, but a gift,
a dark gift for other lives, still on the wing.

Dizzying Work

We were all watching The Pile back in Manhattan,
the smoking ruin, national crime scene,
being taken apart with acetylene torches
and hauled away until it went underground,
and it was a hole again, a place not-there.

Where did all that once was
the Twin Towers, the whole World
Trade Center complex,
that once was Ground Zero, once was, once was…

Once they climbed from that depth, climbed
that ramp back up to street level
where did those trucks rumble off to?

All through the remaining fall, through that first winter,
truckload after truckload came to Fresh Kills,
to people whose job meant pulling on
respirators and protective white suits.
They'd fill sifting machines
and hour after hour stood witness
as the gray rubble and debris tumble by
on never-stopping conveyor belts.

All that motion. Watching
all that passing. The material
always passing made dizzying work.
Anything that might be
something—a Gap bag, an insurance card,
a Fossil watch, a charred sleeve of slides,
—was plucked up out the stream
and placed in black buckets.

Site supervisor James Luongo said,
*You have to be able to look at something
and not see it.* A clump of hair.
A thigh bone. That hand,

its nails manicured. A ceremonial silence
emerged within the machine noise.
Remains were brought
to the refrigerated trailer,
where the Japanese family had left flowers.

In the early days, just afterwards,
a crushed police car was brought to Fresh Kills,
its radio still broadcasting.
No one dared turn it off.

II

Some of us know what

we never thought we'd know—

the sound of 110 stories being told

in gravity's flat voice and the limits

of metaphor: *It sounded like*

what it was, and the taste of metal

like pennies in the mouth

only sweeter, and the color of blood

splashed up on the glass above where

the body, the stranger to me,

the mother, wife, sister, fell—

and what kept us going

was the knowledge that what happened

could never happen.

                  ||

"The World Trade Center is a living symbol
of man's dedication to world peace...

a presentation

> *of man's belief*
> *in humanity*

his need
for individual
dignity

> *his belief*
> *in cooperation*

and through cooperation
his ability to find greatness."

Preserving the Fabric

The snap of the tablecloth
echoed down the stairwell
of the North Tower. Can a sound
sanctify? Do prayers rise or float
or make anything happen?

Between 106 and 107, on a landing,
they laid out a small white field
—one of them flattened the last
olive oil box for a mat—
and made a space for devotion,
an island of spiritual devotion
in the great sea of capitalism.

Muslims from the Ivory Coast,
Morocco, Malaysia—immigrants
and citizens and visitors—
a most American mixture.

Between one floor and another,
between daylight and full night,
between earth and sky,

they gathered, and there
they prayed and together
they broke their fast.

II

"History
          is always
political. It never

          rips in two.
The discontinuities
          of the past

always
        remain
in the whole cloth."

11

The roaring reaches us
before we reach the place where
some say "their souls
are crying,"
           where absence is preserved,
where water pours into squares
and there falls into smaller chambers.

It's not silence but a private veil
of sound, a watery drape
that makes of cityspace a stillness,
one we can inhabit
              if only a moment,
a bead of time to finger lightly.
We inhabit but cannot stay
for we are travelers
who have not yet arrived.

Long after we return to Omaha
or Tokyo, Tallahassee or Seattle,
London, Cincinnati, Istanbul, or Mumbai,
the water will go on falling
and falling
will tell the story of falling.

Notes & Acknowledgements

"Blowback" ("this goes back…") published in *Brain of Forgetting* out of
    Cork, Ireland
—*"a group of mujahedeen" from Chalmers Johnson's* Blowback: The Cost
    and Consequences of American Empire
—*"As I ran north…" by Christine Haughney in* "The Flow of Humanity"
    in At Ground Zero: 25 Stories of Young Reporters Who
Were There. *NY: Thunder's Mouth Press, 2002.*

"The Gambit"
—*Petit section: from* Smithsonian *Nov 2001 "Turning Point" by Robert
    Chelminski. There's also a documentary film,* Man on Wire, *that
    depicts Petit's project, and in the novel* Let the Great World
    Spin, *Colum McCann writes an exquisite scene of him practicing in
    a field. I never found a way to integrate Petit's phrase, "When I see
    oranges, I juggle" into these poems though that kind of compulsion
    animates many aspects of this enterprise.*
— *Zeckendorf + D. Rockefeller section based on material in* City in the Sky:
    The Rise and Fall of the World Trade Towers *by James Glanz and
    Eric Lipton. NY: Henry Holt, 2003.*
—*"our building swayed" from Brian Clark's "Accounts from the South
    Tower"* NYTimes *May 26th, 2002.*

"The Tallest Building in the World"
— *Yamasaki quote in Glanz + Lipton's* City in the Sky
—*"the chain" from Susan L. Woodward "On War and Peace-Building:
    Unfinished Legacy of the 1990s."* Understanding September
    11. *NY: The New Press, 2002. 212-237.*

"The Sweet Unless"
—*The phrase "we will not repeat the evil" is the inscription on the cenotaph
    in Hiroshima's Peace Park.*
—*McKinsey & Co. info from* City in the Sky
— *The term "buildering" is used in Eileen Keerdoja and James C. Jones.
    "Trade Center Stunts"* Newsweek. *7 Nov. 1977. A fine profile of
    Willig's ascent of the South Tower in 1977 was published in*
    Sports Illustrated. *He spent a year preparing for it.*

"Foursquare"

—*Much of the information in this poem is from Glanz + Lipton's* City in the Sky

—*Ada Louise Huxtable's quote from* On Architecture: Collected Reflections on a Century of Change. *NY Walker & Co. 2008. 372-7.*

"Displacement"—*published in* Between the Lines

—*"The line between military…" is from Seyla Benhabib's essay "Unholy Wars, Reclaiming Democratic Virtues" in* Understanding September11.

— *The list of names is distilled from "New York Dispatch: Family Room" in* The New Republic *Oct 1, 2001.*

"Only Descent"

—*"I was standing…doorman." was spoken by Wendell Clyne, "I was waiting a table…" Stuart Nurick in* What We Saw *by CBS News, Simon + Schuster, 2002 recounts the phone interviews with Bryant Gumbal just 4 minutes after the first plane struck.*

—*"In the Stairwell" is a found poem of Bryan Charles' "The Numbers"* in Before and After: Stories from New York; *information about The Bathtub comes from Edith Iglaver's "The Biggest Foundation"* The New Yorker *4 Nov 1972.*

"Sound Waves"

—*Harry Druding is profiled in Glanz + Lipton's* City in the Sky

—*The copter report is from* Above Hallowed Ground: A Photographic Record of September 11, 2001 by the Photographers of the NYC Police Dept.

—*Some sounds are recorded in various accounts in* What We Saw *by CBS News.*

"Echoes"

—*The quote about ambulances is from Scott Pelley, CBS correspondent, in* What We Saw.

—*Information about the Victims' Compensation Fund is from "A Tragic Calculus" by Steven Brill in* Newsweek's *special Dec 2001/Jan 2002 issue. I have not researched how the fund actually operated in the years since.*

"Corrugated"
—*"My initial reaction" is from J. William Frost's speech at the November*
2001 Annual Meeting of the American Friends Service Committee.
His title is "A New War Demands New Responses."
—*The photographer in the gardens of the dead is Joel Meyerowitz, who*
gained access to Ground Zero and took pictures for 9 months.
Sarah Boxer profiled his work in "Even in the Moonscape of
Tragedy, Beauty is in the Eye." NYTimes, *May 23, 2002.*

"Negative Damping"
—*The balsa wood experiment by Dr. Jack Cermak at the Colorado State*
University Fluid Dynamic and Diffusion Lab is described
in Glanz + Lipton City in the Sky.

"Gravity"
—*George Tamano from Glanz + Lipton* City in the Sky
—The Falling Man *is the title of a photo by Richard Drew. The profound*
documentary of the same title explores those who jumped.

"Domino Theory"
— *"An accidental beauty" from photographer Joel Meyerowitz.*
—*Part 3 is a found poem from* Inside 9-11: What Really Happened *by the*
reporters, writers, and editors of Der Spiegel Magazine.
NY: St.Martins, 2001. Translated by Paul De Angelis and Elizabeth
Kaestner.

"Fragments from the Ruins"
—*Many images are from Der Spiegel's* Inside 9/11.

"Diligence"
—*Detail on the perpetrators from* Inside 9/11.

"Möbius Strip"
—*Elevator story is from* Inside 9-11. *The rescuer is Al Smith; the Port*
Authority's acting director is John Paczkowski.
—*Working in the Empire State Building that foggy day during WWII when*
the plane accidentally crashed into it was the woman who would

become George Willig's mother, and the boy would grow up to climb the South Tower in 1977.

"The Afghan Trap"
— *Brzesinski material from William Pitt Rivers, "The Silence after September 11"*
—*"Anything can happen..." by Anna Quindlen "Imagining the Hanson Family" Newsweek, 24 Sept. 2001*
—*"Did Mohammed Atta..." and details about the terrorists are from* Inside 9/11.

"Project Safe Flight"—published in *The Whirlwind Review.*
—*The pet shop escapee monkey peeks through Glanz + Lipton's City in the Sky.*
— *"After September 12" about the rescue dogs from* Above Hallowed Ground.
—*Details about the birds from NYC Audubon Society ("It was hard not to think of souls.") and information about safeguarding birds is from a press release by the Port Authority of New York and New Jersey entitled "Port Authority Takes Steps to Protect Migratory Birds around World Trade Center." September 8, 2000.*
—*Brendan Keim. "9/11 Memorial Lights Trap Thousands of Birds." September 14, 2010.* Wired Science. *wired.com.*

"Dizzying Work" (published in *Up the River*, the publication of Albany Poets)
— *Work at The Hill is from Dan Barry's "Sifting the Last Tons of Sept. 11 Debris"* NYTimes, May 14, 2002
— *"It sounded like what it was" by Michael Wright with Cal Fussman "The Way Down" in* Esquire
—*"The World Trade Center is a living symbol..." by chief architect Minoru Yamasaki from* One Day in History: September 11, 2001.

"Preserving the Fabric" "—published in *Mud Season.*
—*The image of praying in the stairwell comes from a detail in Samuel G. Freeman's* New York Times *article "Muslims and Islam Were Part of the Twin Towers' Life" published on 10 September 2010. He says*

most were employees at Windows on the World who didn't have
time to get to the mosque four blocks away.

—"History / is always / political" from Joanne Meyerowitz "History and
September 11: An introduction" from the special September
2002 issue of The Journal of American History.

—Images of the water falling honor Michael Arad's design for the World
Trade Center memorial, which he calls "Reflecting Absence" and
which is profiled in Martin Filler's "A Masterpiece at Ground Zero"
in the New York Review of Books 27 October 2011.

Edward A. Dougherty was awarded the SUNY Chancellor's Award for Excellence in Scholarship and Creative Activity and has taught English at Corning Community College since 1999. He is the author of four previous books of poetry, the latest of which is *Grace Street* (Cayuga Lake Books), and six chapbooks, including *House of Green Water* (FootHills Publishing). He collaborated with the composer Will Wickham on two productions, *Where Sacred Waters Divide* and *Beyond Any One Life*. His emblems, small abstract artwork with brief poems, were displayed at the Atrium Gallery and the Word and Image Gallery. He is also the co-author, with Scott Minar, of *Exercises for Poets: The Double Bloom* (Pearson/Prentice-Hall).